Soul Alchemy: Verses of the Phoenix Within

Nefretiri McGriff

BookLeaf Publishing

India | USA | UK

ACKNOWLEDGEMENT

I am endlessly grateful to those in my soul tribe. You never allowed me to discount myself and always added value to my quality of life. Your love has been a guiding light that brought me to this point of ascension. A heartfelt thank you to my readers - thank you for allowing these words to touch your hearts and speak to your soul. May they awaken the phoenix within you.

PREFACE

The phoenix is a powerful symbol of transformation, resilience, and rebirth. In this collection, I tell the story of a woman who, like a phoenix, has faced the flames of life's greatest challenges and emerged reborn. Writing this collection was an act of catharsis, a way to give a voice to the quiet strength that lies within us all. As you read, I hope you find solace in her story and recognize the phoenix within yourself, ready to rise from whatever ashes life may leave behind.

Ashes

The chaos of turmoil echoed through the walls,
Heavy breaths and curses filled the halls.
Every weekend, their anger seemed to grow,
Yearning for peace, yet hate would only show.

Dashing out, he drove in wild reverse,
Instinctively, she grabbed her purse.
Dragging her daughter, eyes ablaze with fire,
The tears had stopped; now threats fueled her
ire.
He thought he could just leave it all behind,
Enough was enough; vengeance filled her mind.
I need you to stay in the car and hide,
Remember our game, keep your head low
tonight.

Be quiet, be still,
Everything will be fine, it's the Lord's will.
Silently, her daughter sat in the seat,
Trying to stay awake in the stifling heat.

Embers

In shadows deep, where anger's echoes chase,
A child sits quiet, lost in growing fear.
Her mother's wrath, a storm in endless race,
While father's fading taillights disappear.

Upon the highway's stretch, the night turns cold,
With screeching tires and voices sharp as knives.
She pleads, unheard, as chaos takes its hold,
A witness to the war that wrecks their lives.

But in her heart, a seed of strength takes root,
Though tears may fall and terror grip her soul.
She learns that silence has its own pursuit,
A spark of hope within the dark, her goal.

Though shadows linger, heavy in her mind,
She'll seek the light that's hidden yet to find.

Finding Flames

The night was long, but morning finds her home,
Where echoes of the past begin to fade.
Her mother weeps, the bottle now her friend,
While she prepares for school with silent dread.
She wonders if the day will bring her peace,
Or if her heart will ever truly mend.

She pulls her uniform, its folds unbend,
Yet can't erase the memory of home.
The place that should bring comfort, love, and
peace,
Now fills her with a heavy, lingering dread.
At school, she hopes to feel the tension fade,
But finds no solace in the faces of her friends.

Her thoughts stray far from lessons to her friend,
The fleeting hope that life might somehow
mend.
But every thought returns to growing dread,
The fear of what she'll face again at home.
Her teacher's voice, a murmur, starts to fade,
As she slips deeper, searching for some peace.

In dreams, she drifts where there is only peace,
Where laughter fills the space of every friend.
But daydreams are a thin and fleeting fade,
The bell rings, jolting her from thoughts that
mend.
She wonders how she'll ever call it home,
A place where shadows fall with constant dread.

At last, the school day ends, the final dread
Is met with joy—a brother's face, her peace.
He takes her hand, and for a moment, home
Is far away, and she is with a friend.
In his embrace, the wounds begin to mend,
The pain of morning starts to gently fade.

She knows that this reprieve will surely fade,
That every step brings closer thoughts of dread.
But here, with him, her fragile heart can mend,
Can feel, if only briefly, tender peace.
She treasures every moment with her friend,
Forgets the broken world that waits at home.

The night will come, and with it shadows fade,
Yet dread still lingers, even with a friend.
But peace can bloom, and even she can mend.

Smoldering Silence

In the quiet of the night, she mourns alone,
Her tears fall like the autumn rain's descent.
The brother she lost, her heart's heavy stone,
Taken before she could say her lament.

She sits in silence, burdened by her weight,
Her anger, a storm that lashes with no end.
Her mother's choice to keep her from the gate,
Left her with wounds that time will never mend.

Her instrument, a solace in the band,
Where every chord releases some despair.
The band director's words like a guiding hand,
A reminder that her name holds worth and care.

Yet the rage spills over in her school's halls,
As she battles shadows of her parents' brawls.

Cinders of Hope

She stands at the threshold of high school,
her body heavier with the weight of years,
the remnants of middle school memories
clinging
like the fabric of her too-tight clothes.

The anger has softened now,
a quiet ember instead of a roaring flame.
The house no longer shakes
with her parents' battles,
their divorce drawing a line between them—
yet the cracks still whisper in the walls,
and she hears them late at night,
echoing through the hollow spaces
where love once tried to grow.

She no longer rages
but feels the pinch of every pound,
a reminder of what's been carried—
of silence, of confusion, of betrayal.
Her reflection offers little solace,
a body she barely recognizes,
a heart still learning how to heal.

But there is music,
and in it, she finds herself again,
her fingers dancing on keys,
her breath steadying on the mouthpiece.
The band room becomes her sanctuary,
the place where the world quiets,
where she can name herself
without needing to know
who she'll be in the morning.

She walks through the halls of her new school,
her head held higher,
her feet still learning the rhythm
of standing alone.

And though her father's absence cuts,
though her mother's silence still aches,
she is not without hope—
it burns softly, a cinder,
beneath the weight of everything she's been,
everything she's lost.

She lets it smolder,
a small light,
enough to carry her through
another day,
enough to remind her
that there is still a fire inside her
that belongs to no one
but herself.

Kindling the Spirt

They told her to shrink, to let her body fall in line—
She shed the weight, but her heart was heavy all the time.

No more band room solace, no music to hold her tight—
She wandered through days, searching for a new rhyme.

A boy with soft eyes, a voice like summer rain,

Whispered her name, made her feel like love's
prime.

He showed her hands, tracing skin like fragile
glass,
Teaching her touch, a new language, a secret
sign.

In the mirror, she saw a stranger, beautiful and
thin—
But the girl she once was stood watching, behind
the shine.

Her spirit stirred, kindled by his gentle heat,
But what burns fast, leaves embers over time.

She wondered, in the quiet, what part of her was
true—
For she offered only hugs and kisses, yet he
wanted more than she knew.

Betrayed.

He spoke in whispers, promises of light,
Ending her innocence with shadows of night.

Trust was a gift he took with ease,
Oblivious to the damage, he brought her to her
knees.
Only now she sees the cost of the deceit,
Keeping her heart trapped in silent defeat.

Multiple aches from the force that stung,
Yielding to a pain that's left her numb and
young.

Illusions shattered by a false embrace,
Never prepared for this cruel disgrace.
Nightmares echo with every false vow,

Overcome by the truth, she's learning now.
Caught in the web of his twisted schemes,
Echoes of betrayal haunt her dreams.
Navigating the wreckage, her soul bruised and
scarred,
Cherishing fragments of hope that are hard.
Ending her days in a silent guard.

Rising Heat (an Ode)

O fire within, you who have carried her
through—
The weight of a life in constant motion,
From one apartment to the next,
Where walls change like seasons,
Yet the burdens remain the same.
Her mother's grief, a river that never dries,
Washing over her, pulling her deeper
Into the role of healer, mender, caretaker,
Before her own wounds could ever close.

O girl of rising heat, your father's love flickers
Like a candle in a storm,
Distant, unreliable, a warmth that never lingers.
Yet you, with the strength of mountains,
Have learned to build where nothing stands.
You pick up the stones of your mother's pain,

And carry them, though they weigh heavy,
Turning them into steps
Toward a life you craft with your own hands.

O warrior of two jobs and sleepless nights,
Where a heart once soft now grow calloused,
And school remains a light,
A beacon in the fog of your days.
Your friends, new and bright as stars,
Help you to shine, to rise beyond the noise,
And in their laughter, you find
Pieces of the girl you've yet to become.

O strength that burns, you rise like the sun—
Each day a step further from the ashes
Of broken homes and broken hearts.
You bear the scars of a past
That tried to hold you down,
But your spirit, relentless,
Refuses to yield to the weight of it all.
Through the heat, you've become a force,
Forging a future
From the embers of all that's come undone.

O rising heat,
You are the flame that cannot be tamed,
The girl who will not stay in the shadows.
In your work, your studies, your laughter,
You climb higher, burning brighter,

With each step forward,
You rise, unshaken,
Beyond the doors that tried to keep you bound.

Flames of Resilience

Part I

She walks the halls of her new life, alone,
But not afraid—the dorm lights flicker bright.
Her world, once filled with shadows, now has
grown
Into a place where dreams can take their flight.
New friends, like stars, have gathered at her
side,
They laugh and whisper secrets of the night.
She learns of womanhood with cautious pride,
How strength and softness blend in perfect light.
The walls are thin, but her resolve is strong,
A scholarship her lifeline and her fire.
She works despite the echo of their song—
Her parents' pleas to focus, their one desire.
But she must climb, must build her way alone,
This independence is her cornerstone.

Part II

One night, a man with eyes too dark to trust
Whispered sweet lies she once had heard before.
She felt the heat of want, the pull of lust,
But knew too well the cost behind the door.
Her heart, once torn, now bears the scars of
strength,
She dodged his grasp, her spirit holding fast.
For she had learned, at last, to go the length—
To stand and fight for peace that's built to last.
Now thriving in her world of books and thought,
She works and studies, carving out her space.
Her parents' words, though kind, can hold her
not—
She finds her worth in freedom's fierce embrace.
The flames of resilience burn deep inside,
A woman now, she walks with steady stride.

Phoenix Ascending

The moment of flight didn't come
as she expected—
it came with a fall,
a quiet descent back home,
where familiar walls
welcomed her with silence.
The dorm felt like freedom,
but freedom, it seems,
had a price.

She returns,
not in defeat,
but in the slow unraveling of what she thought
she'd left behind.
Her body, once strong, now betrays her,
hunger becoming something else—

a way to control the uncontrollable,
to shrink the chaos inside.

She counts calories like secrets,
measures her worth in the mirror's gaze,
each bite a battle between who she is
and who she's afraid to become.
Her mother notices,
her father says nothing—
they tread lightly, unsure of the girl
who left, bright with dreams,
and returned, a shadow of that fire.

But she is no stranger to ashes.
She's burned before,
has felt the weight of wings too heavy to lift,
and yet—
she knows rebirth,
knows the way embers glow beneath the skin,
waiting for air,
waiting for breath.

The hunger is not the end of her story.
She feels the pull of the flame deep within,
a flicker that refuses to die,
even as the world tightens its grip.
Her body, now a battleground,
will rise again,
will learn to heal in its own time.

She may be home,
but this time, it's different.
The woman in the mirror
is still finding her way,
still learning that rebirth
is not a single moment,
but a series of sparks—
each one a choice to keep going,
to keep rising.

And so she ascends,
slowly, steadily,
her wings singed but unbroken,
her soul a phoenix
emerging, once again,
from the ashes.

Wings of Fire

She sought the light in places long denied,
Where shadows once had claimed her frailest
part.
With tender hands, she healed the war inside,
Rebuilding strength from fragments of her heart.
Her body, now her own, began to heal,
No longer bound by hunger's silent chains.
She found new purpose, helping others feel
The power born from overcoming pains.

Now foster children find their way to her,
And young girls, lost like she had once been too,
Are lifted by her words, her hands, her care—
Their broken wings begin to mend anew.

With wings of fire, she soars into the sky,
Her strength reclaimed, her spirit lifted high.

Fires of Forgiveness

She reaches out, her heart softening at last,
To mend the broken bridge between her and
him.
Her father's anger flares, a fire that won't fade—
He claims she gives more love to those who've
hurt her less,
To siblings and mother, where his love remains
denied.
But still, she tries, her spirit yearning for peace.

For years, she's sought the quiet calm of peace,
Letting go of past hurts that lingered too long at
last.
But with him, it's harder—his love feels denied,

As though the flames of anger have consumed
him.
She can't explain why she's given more to the
rest,
Why the scars they left behind have slowly
begun to fade.

For ten long years, their voices seem to fade,
The silence between them grows wider than
peace.
She finds forgiveness for herself and the rest,
But her father—he is the one challenge left at
last.
She wonders if the years apart have changed
him,
If his heart, like hers, still longs for what was
denied.

Then one day, after the years of calls not tried,
She reaches out to him, her fears begin to fade.
She sits with him, hoping to know the man he's
become,
To find the spark of love beneath the chaos, the
peace.
For a moment, they laugh, the tension gone at
last,
A flicker of hope among the pain they'd known
too long with the rest.

But the fires of the past still burn, the hurt won't
rest—
Just as they start to heal, the connection is
denied.
COVID comes, and their bond is broken again at
last,
The distance between them now too deep to
fade.
She learns to carry on, to make her own peace,
And to accept that she may never fully know
him.

In time, she forgives herself for failing him,
Forgives the ones who left her with wounds to
rest.
The fires of forgiveness become her peace,
She no longer waits for love that's been denied.
Her heart is lighter now, the pain begins to fade,
For she has freed herself from the past at last.

At last, she soars beyond the ashes of him—
The anger fades, forgiveness finds its rest.
Denied no more, she's found her lasting peace.

Reigniting Peace

She once believed her mother's hands were soft,
But time reveals the scars beneath their grace.
Now bound in care, she feels the heavy cost—
Her own life sacrificed for her mother's face.
She sees the flaws that once were veiled in light,
Her innocence lost in the harshness of truth.

It shakes her, this new and bitter truth,
That even her mother's love has edges, not soft.
The memories of childhood twist in new light,
She sees her role, the pain, the mounting cost.
The weight of duty written on her face,
Her own needs buried for her mother's grace.

But how could she have missed the cracks in
grace,
The faults that lived beneath a masked truth?
Her mother, too, has worn a broken face,
A life of hardship that never felt soft.
And yet, the years have taught her what it cost,
To always see her mother in pure light.

Her spirit dims beneath this glaring light,
As caregiving pulls at her sense of grace.
She wonders how much longer she can bear the
cost—
To abandon her dreams for this daily truth.
Where once she found love's burden to be soft,
Now weariness is etched upon her face.

And so she searches for a clearer face,
One free from the shadows, full of healing light.
She turns inward, seeking something soft,
A source of strength, a deeper kind of grace.
Her soul awakens to a higher truth,
That self-care, too, is worth any cost.

With time, she learns the balance of that cost,
No longer lost in the lines of another's face.
She builds her life upon a truer truth,
A peace reignited, burning pure and light.
She forgives herself, and with this act of grace,

Finds softness in her heart, where she's been
soft.

The cost of peace is knowing its true light,
Facing her own face with tenderness and grace,
For in that truth, she rises free and soft.

Echoes of Ash (Her POV)

The echoes of ash still linger,
soft whispers of where I've been,
faint traces of the flames that once consumed
me.
I walk through the dust of my past
and gather what's left,
not in sorrow, but in reverence—
for every scar has its story,
every burn its wisdom.

I used to think
the fire was my enemy,
that its heat would hollow me out,
leave me empty.
But now, I see—
the blaze was not my undoing,

it was my beginning.
The flames didn't destroy me,
they shaped me,
molding the raw edges of my soul
into something solid,
something strong.

From the ashes, I rose,
not unscathed,
but unbroken.

There are lessons only fire can teach—
the power of letting go,
of surrendering to what can't be controlled.
I've learned that healing doesn't mean erasing
the hurt,
but carrying it with grace,
letting it live in me
without letting it rule me.

I no longer fear the flames.
I've learned to dance with them,
to let their heat remind me
of what I've survived,
of the power I hold.

The echoes of ash
are not the end,
they are the beginning of the next fire,

the next rise.
I carry them with me,
a quiet strength,
a reminder
that I am more than the girl who was burned.
I am the woman
who walks through flames
and emerges whole.

The past is there,
etched in the smoke that curls behind me,
but it no longer binds me.
I carry its wisdom,
but I choose my own fire now,
and I know—
I will always rise.

Inner Blaze

A shift in life, a brand-new path begun,
But shadows fall as news of illness spreads.
Stage one, they say, and yet the war's not won—
A fight within her womb, where dreams are
shed.
Resentment stirs, for years she gave her all,
To children unloved, now faced with barren
ground.
Her tears, a silent storm, begin to fall,
As hope seems lost, and peace is nowhere found.

But deep within, a flame begins to rise,
A fire she's known, though buried, still it glows.
She finds her strength beneath the tearful skies,
The blaze within her heart forever grows.

Though fate may change, she walks with
burning grace,
Her inner fire, her guiding light, her place.

Burned But Unbroken

She wears her scars like armor, burned but
unbroken,
Each wound a testament to strength, never
forsaken.

The flames of her past have tried to consume
her,
Yet she rises each time, from ashes unspoken.

Her body may carry the marks of her battles,
But her spirit shines through, a fire awoken.

Setbacks may come, but they fuel her desire,
With every fall, she stands taller—unyielding,
unbroken.

In the quiet of night, she recalls the pain,
But in the dawn's light, she's radiant, outspoken.

Burned but unbroken, she walks through the fire,
Her heart ablaze, her courage never shaken.

Fire and Grace

In her third year as an entrepreneur,
life is a landscape reshaped by shadows and
light.
She walks through a world altered by a virus,
her body a vessel that has known the grip of
COVID twice.

The hustle of days, the rush of nights—
it all feels different now.
Her strength, once a blaze that would consume,
has found its counterpoint in the softness of
experience.

The fire within her still burns,
but it dances with a new grace,
a rhythm learned from navigating the ashes
of her own fragility.

She moves with a balance
between fierce determination and gentle resolve,
her hands steady on the wheel of her dreams,
her heart open to the quiet lessons of survival.

In the aftermath of illness and challenge,
she finds harmony in her duality—
the fierce spirit that drives her forward,
and the tender soul that embraces her humanity.

Fire and grace—
these are the forces that shape her,
that guide her through the uncertainties,
through the echoes of what was, and the promise
of what is yet to come.

She is a testament to resilience,
a living proof that strength can be tender,
that passion can be calm,
and that even after the hardest trials, she rises
with a spirit ignited and a heart at peace.

Eternal Flame

She almost talked herself out of dreams, where
flames could burn,
Yet her spirit ignored the doubts, letting inner
fire churn.

In the quiet of hesitation, the voice of fear would
claim,
But she moved past those shadows, igniting her
eternal flame.

The world outside seemed vast, her talents
hidden in the dark,
Yet she stepped into the light, her courage a bold
mark.

Resilience shaped her path, through trials that
seemed unkind,
Her heart held a flame so fierce, a brilliance
redefined.

Limiting beliefs tried to silence her spark,
But she embraced her power, her light no longer
stark.

Success came as a testament to the fire she'd
tended well,
Each victory a testament, each story a tale to tell.

Eternal in its radiance, her flame cannot be
quenched,
She rises ever brighter, her spirit never drenched.

Phoenix's Heart

In the heart of her being, a fire now burns bright,
No longer a whisper, but a call to the world.
The Phoenix has risen, her spirit alive with
purpose,
Her gifts, no longer hidden, shine through her
vibrant soul.
She steps into the light, her presence both bold
and true,
A beacon of strength, her heart's strength
renewed.

The strength of her heart is now a radiant force,
Alive with purpose, each moment a vibrant
dance.

She shares her gifts with the world, no longer in
secret,
Her voice rings clear, her spirit unbound.
Her presence is celebrated, the world now fully
awake,
And in this light, she finds peace and grace.

Her father, once distant, now sees the change in
her,
Their paths converge in the warmth of a
reconciled truth.
She witnesses his peace, a reflection of her own,
And wonders how it feels to be a daddy's girl.
With courage anew, she takes a chance on this
love,
Her heart open, seeking the bond she's never
known.

Living out loud, she embraces the bond and its
light,
Her father's presence now a part of her vibrant
story.
She's no longer a secret, but a force in her own
right,
A Phoenix whose heart knows both strength and
grace.
Her purpose, her fire, both fierce and alive,
Echoes through the peace she finds, reaching for
the sky.

In the heart of her being, she is unafraid,
No longer hidden, her presence an appreciated
gift.
With each step forward, she feels the full
embrace
Of a life lived boldly, purposefully, and bright.
She makes amends, explores the love of a
daddy's girl,
And finds that her heart, now strong, is forever
renewed.

Soaring From Ash

She rises, not just from the remnants of
yesterday,
but from the very essence of her own
transformation.
Her past, now a whisper in the wind,
a collection of lessons turned into wings.
She soars above the landscape of her former self,
a phoenix freed from the constraints of what
once was.

In the light of her ascent,
she finds clarity in the simple truths—
that her energy belongs to what nourishes her
soul,

to the vibrant dance of the present moment,
to the harmony between grace and power.
Her life, once a muted echo, now sings with
authenticity.

No longer weighed down by the ashes of regret,
she embraces her future with open arms,
each day a canvas for her unspoken dreams.
Her spirit is attuned to the rhythm of the
universe,
a symphony of being that resonates with the
divine.
She moves through the world with a knowing
grace,
her presence a testament to the strength she's
forged.

Every breath she takes is a celebration of what
is,
an acknowledgment of the journey she's
traveled.
In her wake, she leaves a trail of light,
a beacon for others who seek to rise from their
own shadows.
She is unapologetic in her truth,
living each moment as a testament to her power
and grace.

Soaring from the ash, she dances through her
life,
each step a manifestation of her spiritual
evolution.
She gives her energy to what truly matters,
her heart a vessel of both strength and serenity.
In this new chapter, she is wholly alive,
embracing her path with unwavering
authenticity.

Here, in this space between what was and what
will be,
she finds her center, her purpose, her joy.
The ashes of her past have become the soil
from which her true self has emerged.
And as she soars, she does so with a fierce,
graceful freedom,
a testament to the fire within her that can never
be extinguished.

Blaze of Glory

Born from the ashes of a life once torn,
Lifting her wings, she greets each new dawn.
Accepting the flaws of those who caused her
pain,
Zealously rising above, she breaks every chain.
Every wound once carved into her soul, now
healed,

Open to the world, her true power revealed.
Forgiveness flows like an amber ocean's tide,
Guided by spirit, no longer needing to hide.
Light radiates from her heart, bold and true,
Others find healing in the warmth she imbues.
Reaching new heights, she has found her way,
Yesterday's storms have led to today's brighter
day.